COLONIAL PEOPLE

The Carpenter

MICHAEL BURGAN

Cavendish Square

New York

Published in 2014 by Cavendish Square Publishing, LLC
303 Park Avenue South, Suite 1247, New York, NY 10010

Copyright © 2014 by Cavendish Square Publishing, LLC

First Edition

Website: cavendishsq.com

CPSIA Compliance Information: Batch #WS13CSQ

All websites were available and accurate when this book was sent to press.

Library of Congress Cataloging-in-Publication Data
Burgan, Michael.
The carpenter / Michael Burgan.
p. cm. — (Colonial people)
Includes bibliographical references and index.
Summary: "Explores the life of a colonial carpenter and his importance to the community, as well as everyday life
responsibilities, and social practices during that time"—Provided by publisher.
ISBN 978-1-60870-411-8 (hardcover) — ISBN 978-1-62712-045-6 (paperback) — ISBN 978-1-60870-984-7 (ebook)
1. Carpenters—United States—History—17th century—Juvenile literature. 2. Carpenters—United States—History—18th
century—Juvenile literature. 3. United States—Social life and customs—To 1775—Juvenile literature. 4. United States—
History—Colonial period, ca. 1600-1775—Juvenile literature. I. Title. II. Series.
HD8039.C32U627 2013
694.0973'0903—dc23
2011028341

Editor: Peter Mavrikis
Art Director: Anahid Hamparian
Series Designer: Kay Petronio

Photo research by Marybeth Kavanagh

Cover photo by Edouard Amable Onslow/Musee Crozatier, Le Puy-en-Velay, France/Giraudon/The Bridgeman Art Library

The photographs in this book are used by permission and through the courtesy of: *Getty Images*: MPI, 4; Danita Delimont/
Gallo Images, 27; *The Image Works*: Print Collector/HIP, 8; *The Bridgeman Art Library*: Piedmont Room, Guildford County
North Carolina, c.1766 by American School (18th century) Museum of Early Southern Decorative Arts, USA, 11; *North
Wind Picture Archives*: 14, 15, 35, 43; *Alamy*: Adrian Davies, 18; Pat & Chuck Blackley, 22; Philip Scalia, 31; David Bleeker
Photography.com, 34; *Corbis*: Michael Freeman, 26; *The Colonial Williamsburg Foundation*: 33, 37, 39; *SuperStock*: Robert
Harding Picture Library, 41

Printed in the United States of America

CONTENTS

ONE

Building a New Nation

About five hundred years ago, Europeans began coming to North America. People from Spain, England, the Netherlands, France, and other countries settled in what is now the United States. In the east, they found huge areas of land shaped by thousands of years of human development: open meadows, tall stands of thinned woods, and dense forests on the slopes of the Appalachians. In other areas, such as the hot deserts of the Southwest, few trees grew. Wherever the Europeans settled, one thing was true: they needed shelter right away, to protect them from harsh weather and possible attacks by enemies.

Helping to fill that need were carpenters. Some carpenters came on the ships that carried farmers, soldiers, traders, and others seeking a better life in America. Some carpenters learned their craft once they reached the **colonies**. In either case,

Using carpentry skills, the settlers at Jamestown built this small village in little more than a year.

carpenters often had many jobs, using their hands, their tools, and wood to build whatever their customers wanted.

The First Carpenters

The most detailed records of colonial carpenters come from the English colonies along the Atlantic Ocean. Forests were especially plentiful there, and the settlers soon began to use wood to build their homes. Diaries, newspapers, and public records offer clues about the lives of carpenters. And some of their buildings still stand, showing how some carpenters worked.

In 1607, England set up its first permanent colony in Jamestown, Virginia. For several months, the settlers lived in tents or simple huts. Then, Captain John Smith, one of the leaders of the group, ordered a carpenter to take men into the forest and cut down trees to build a fort and houses. The carpenter taught them how to turn the wood into **clapboard**, which was often used in England to build houses. Within a few years, the settlers had constructed several dozen buildings surrounded by a wooden wall 15 feet high.

Carpenters did more than build houses. The Virginians and the settlers of Massachusetts also relied on ships' carpenters, or **shipwrights**, to repair any problems with their vessels. In

Carpenters in Jamestown

Records show that several carpenters traveled with Captain Smith to Virginia. Some of them were dead by the time Smith ordered the settlers to begin building permanent homes. The settlers battled starvation during their first months in Virginia. By the end of 1608, more ships had arrived from England with food and new settlers. Soon after, a carpenter named John Laydon married one of the new arrivals, Anne Burras. It was the first English wedding in Virginia.

England, these carpenters helped build the ships, which were made mostly of wood. They carried on that role in the colonies, too.

In Plymouth, Massachusetts, the **Pilgrims** arrived with both a house carpenter and a ship's carpenter. William Bradford was governor of the colony in 1626. He wrote that the shipwright had died, but not before passing on some of his skills to the house carpenter. The house carpenter offered to take one of the existing small boats and make it larger. Then the Pilgrims could use it to trade goods with Indian tribes in Maine, more than 100 miles away. Bradford described how the carpenter "lengthened her [the small boat] some 5 or 6 foot, and strengthened her with **timbers**, and so built her up, and laid a deck on her, and so made her a convenient and wholesome vessel, very fit and comfortable for their use. . . ."

North of Plymouth, in Massachusetts Bay, English settlers known as Puritans also relied on the skills of carpenters. From the earliest days of the colonies, carpenters were often in short supply. The ones who came to America could usually find steady work in cities and larger towns. And they could earn more money than other workers who were not in such demand. In Massachusetts Bay, the wealthiest settlers could afford to pay whatever price the carpenters asked, but poorer families could not. The Puritan leaders responded by placing a limit on how much a carpenter could charge per day.

In later years, carpenters and their customers had a number of ways to set fees. Some carpenters charged by the day, while others gave a fixed price for

Carpenters of the 18th century used various saws, such as the one shown here.

an entire job. A third method used another carpenter, called a measurer, to measure how much work the carpenter did. The customer and the carpenter agreed ahead of time on the rate for each unit of work completed, and they accepted the measurer's totals of how much work had been done.

In Spanish Lands

Spain had colonies in what became the United States decades before the English arrived. But records from the earliest days do not say much about carpenters. And in some areas, the settlers built many buildings out of adobe. This mixture of clay, straw, and water was used as a building material by Pueblo peoples, who were accomplished builders. Still, Spanish buildings had some wood, and carpenters had a role to play. At times, the Spanish taught carpentry skills to the Indians they met and, in turn, learned the Indians' building methods. A visitor to Florida in 1675 was impressed with the wooden churches some Indians had built. And in California, Indian carpenters worked at the missions, where Roman Catholic priests lived and taught the Indians about Christianity. By the 1820s, Spanish soldiers relied on the Indians to do carpentry at their forts.

Skills of All Kinds

House carpenters did more than make the frames and roofs of buildings. Carpenters were also sometimes called joiners, a name for **artisans** who assembled wooden items, such as doors, windows, stairs, and basic furniture. Some carpenters had even greater skills. They could make cabinets and detailed furniture for the homes they built. Carpenters were also like today's architects, as they often designed the house or building they were going to construct. Some were also what are known today as general contractors. They hired other skilled craftspeople and watched over their work. These artisans included bricklayers and masons—experts in building with stone. If a house had a slate roof, the carpenter might call in a mason, or a **thatcher** if a roof made of plant stalks was required.

Carpenters made extra money building a variety of wooden items. Some built coffins used to bury the dead. Others made barrels, a job normally performed by artisans called coopers. And a few carpenters ran lumberyards, selling wood that others used in their own building projects. For some carpenters, working with wood was not even their main job. In rural areas, farmers could not always find carpenters to meet their building needs. Many taught themselves basic carpentry skills. Some carpenters who could not find work, such as those in parts of the South, turned to farming for part of their income.

Traveling from town to town was a way of life for carpenters who could not find enough work in one location. The carpenters might take out ads, such as this one from the *Maryland Journal* of

Skilled carpenters made furniture, such as tables, chairs, and cabinets.

1774: "There is arrived in this town, a person well recommended as a house carpenter and joiner, and in drawing plans. . . ." At times, these traveling carpenters competed with local farmers who had carpentry skills, especially after the harvest was complete.

Wherever they worked and whatever they did, carpenters offered customers a special set of skills. The best carpenters were well trained, part of an old system that traced its roots back to England hundreds of years before Jamestown was founded. Let's take a closer look at the lives of colonial carpenters.

TWO

Becoming a Carpenter

Hammering nails or wooden pegs, shaping wood with different tools, cutting trees for timber—all these tasks, and more, made up a typical day for a carpenter. But in reality, few days were exactly the same for any one carpenter. Carpenters had different duties, depending on where they lived or the skills they possessed.

The Guild System

For centuries, English carpenters learned their craft through the guild system. This system had three levels. At the bottom was the **apprentice**, who signed a contract with a master carpenter. The master carpenter ran his own business. The apprentice agreed to work for the master so he could learn carpentry skills. Above the apprentice were journeymen carpenters, who were free to travel and take on jobs wherever they liked. After a certain number of years of training, an apprentice became a journeyman.

This apprentice planes a block of wood, to make it smooth.

This same system was used in the American colonies, though with some slight changes. In England, the guild for any skilled artisan made sure members knew their craft. In America, the system was more informal. In the South in particular, a person could call himself a master carpenter even if he was not. Few people would know the difference, since so few master carpenters lived there to challenge another carpenter's skills.

Apprenticeship was also a little different in the colonies. There, apprentices signed contracts, called **indentures**, that required them to work for a master for four or five years. The contracts were typically seven years long in England, though some ran that long in America as well. Across England and the colonies, all carpenter's apprentices faced a challenging life as they prepared for their new career.

A Family Affair

Not all American carpenters learned their skills through the apprentice system created in Europe. Some could learn basic skills by reading guidebooks. Most of these were written by English experts. More commonly, a carpenter passed on his skills to his son. On Long Island, in New York, the Dominy family was famous for its skilled carpenters and woodworkers. Nathaniel Dominy III started the tradition in the mid-1700s. His son and grandson of the same name continued the family's skilled work with wood. The Dominy home had a workshop attached to it, and it passed on through the generations. The family had a wide range of skills. They made clocks, wooden wheels, cabinets, and tools, and at times they even repaired guns.

The first step in building homes was cutting down trees, as these Pilgrims do.

The Apprentice

Perhaps a boy of only thirteen or so, a carpenter's apprentice left his home to go live with the master carpenter. His family arranged the contract in the hope of giving their son a well-paying career. During the seventeenth century, children in Connecticut were forced to become apprentices if their parents could not keep them from becoming "rude, stubborn, and unruly." In those cases, town officials took the children to "place them with some masters for years, boys till they come to twenty one. . . ." The colony wanted to make sure the children had useful careers, even if their parents could not provide it.

With the typical indenture, the master promised to teach the boy all of a carpenter's skills and provide food, a room, and clothing. The carpenter also taught the apprentice how to read, write, and do arithmetic and **geometry**. Carpenters had to be able to write and understand contracts, draw up building plans, and read manuals that helped them improve their skills. The math was useful for keeping track of expenses and wages and for understanding the geometry of building. **Rafters** and supporting pieces of wood called braces had to be set at certain angles or be of certain widths to carry the load of a house.

In return, the apprentice promised to assist the master in all areas of the job. He needed the master's permission to leave the workshop and was expected to avoid bad habits such as excessive drinking and gambling that would hamper his work. The apprentice also promised not to reveal any secrets of the trade to anyone who was not a carpenter.

Working with the master, the apprentice faced long hours—up to sixteen per day. Apprentices did some of the hardest physical work—dragging and cutting logs to make lumber. Then they learned how to cut the piece to the right size for any job. An apprentice might also plumb a wall—make sure it was straight—then learn how to cut a mortise or tenon at the end of a board or beam. To make a tenon, the apprentice cut off some of the wood at the end of the piece, leaving a square peg slightly smaller in width than the rest of the board. This peg would fit snugly in the hole—the mortise—cut in the end of another board. More likely, the apprentice watched the master cut the mortise and tenon. The apprentice then cut wooden pegs called treenails that held the tenon in the mortise.

Over the years, the apprentice learned all aspects of carpentry. When an apprentice's contract was up, a master might ask his apprentice to show an example of his work, to prove he had truly learned his craft.

Log Cabins

While English carpenters often used mortise and tenons for their buildings, carpenters from Sweden and Finland favored a different style. Starting in the 1630s, Swedes and Finns came to New Sweden—what is now Delaware, southern New Jersey, and southeastern Pennsylvania. They introduced the log cabin to America. For this kind of home, the carpenter cut notches near both ends of all his logs. The notch from one log went into the notch of the other. Log cabins required few tools, since there were no nails and little precise cutting. Truly skilled workers, working quickly, could put together a small log cabin in only a few days. A man working by himself might need a few weeks. Later, other settlers borrowed the design of the log cabin and took it with them as they moved farther west across America.

Log cabins are still built today, though many come from kits.

An apprentice might ask to be freed from his contract early, as Thomas Millard did. He was a carpenter's apprentice in Springfield, Massachusetts, during the 1640s. The master agreed, but he refused to give Millard the money he would have received if he had completed his apprenticeship. The master, William Pynchon, did give Millard some new clothes. Masters were usually required to do this when the contract ended, and some carpenters gave their apprentices tools to help them start their careers.

On the Run

Not all apprentice carpenters liked their work—or their masters. Newspapers sometimes ran ads placed by carpenters looking for apprentices who had run away. Here is part of one ad that ran in a Virginia newspaper in 1750:

> "Ran away . . . an apprentice, about 20 years of age, named Richard Green, a house carpenter and joiner by trade, about 5 feet 9 inches high, slim-made . . . freckled and very talkative . . . also stole two horses."

This servant likely had acquired significant carpentry skills and tried to pass himself as a journeyman to work for his own wages.

On large **plantations**, which were centered in the South, carpenters also took on African American apprentices. These were slaves belonging to the plantation owner. With many buildings and fences to build and repair, plantations had almost endless carpentry needs. The slave owner saved money by training his own carpenters, rather than hiring them. Once a slave carpenter was skilled enough, the owner could hire him out to other farmers, giving the plantation another source of money. Ship's carpenters were the most highly prized, since fewer men, black or white, had their skills.

At times, slave artisans could keep some of the money they earned, helping them buy their own freedom. Records from the eighteenth century show free black carpenters living and working in Maryland. In some cases, slave carpenters ran away with some of their tools, hoping to pass themselves off as free while they made a living.

The Journeyman

As the name suggests, journeymen carpenters often traveled to find work. The master carpenter who trained the journeyman might ask him to stay in his shop. The journeyman was free to do so, or hit the road in search of something better. Those journeymen who traveled offered their skills to master carpenters who needed extra help on big projects. If masters were in short supply, a journeyman might be able to convince a customer to let him take the job. A journeyman could go wherever he could find the highest wage or the job that best matched his skills. For most jobs, he received a room and meals as well as his wages.

For most journeymen, the goal was to make enough money to set up their own shop. Some had to borrow money to make this dream come true. Becoming a master meant greater income and a chance to settle down and start a family. But not all journeymen became masters. Those who did learned that running a carpentry or woodworking shop was a full-time business, not just a craft.

The Master Carpenter

The master carpenter dealt with the clients, sought projects, hired others to help, and bought supplies. At times, he laid out the basic plans and let others do the harder work. In some cases, friends and relatives of the client might help with putting up the frames of a house or barn. If the master did all the framing and roofing, he might leave the inside work for the client to complete over the winter. A master with woodworking skills could build the more decorative items for a home, such as molding around floors or ceilings.

For a time, several Northern cities, such as Boston and New York, required all master craftsmen to pay a fee to set up a shop. But by the mid-1700s, that requirement faded. The cities wanted the skills of carpenters and other artisans.

A sign like this one in Williamsburg, Virginia, told customers they were outside a furniture-maker's shop.

The South and some other areas had a certain kind of master carpenter—the master builder. This title was not used in the old English guild system. The American master builders were the best at their craft, with the biggest shops. They were also sometimes called "undertakers," because they would undertake, or agree to complete, major jobs. These could include building churches or public buildings. One of the most famous master builders of the South was Benjamin Powell of Williamsburg, Virginia. In the eighteenth century, Williamsburg was the capital of the colony, and it had many beautiful buildings. Powell oversaw the construction of the public hospital and the rebuilding of the local jail. Southern master builders relied on their own slaves or ones they hired to do much of the work on their projects.

The Shipwright

A ship's carpenter would also usually learn his trade by becoming an apprentice, then working his way up to a master. Jesse Cook was a seventeen-year-old shipwright's apprentice from North Carolina. In the indenture he signed, he promised "his said master he shall faithfully serve and all his lawful commands everywhere gladly obey."

Shipwrights had to be precise with their work. A hole in the roof or walls of a house would only make the residents a little wet. But a hole in a ship could mean death for a crew far out at sea.

In the earliest colonial times, shipwrights made full models of the ships they were going to build. Later, they worked from written plans and partial models. Building a ship was harder than building a home because a ship had curves. Shipwrights tried to find trees with curves that matched what they were looking for, and cut the wood from them. Many of the pieces of wood were held together with copper or bronze bolts. These metals would not be damaged by the water.

When the shipwright finished putting the wood together, men known as caulkers took over. They sealed the spaces between the wood to make sure water did not get in. The caulkers used rope, which they covered with pitch—a sticky, black substance that came from trees.

Whether shipwrights, journeymen, or masters, carpenters used their skills in various ways. Their talents kept them busy as the American colonies grew.

THREE

Techniques and Tools

Although he was often asked to do many things, the typical house carpenter focused on building homes and other small buildings. The task might begin with dragging logs to the building site. In the early colonial days, the carpenter turned round logs into square beams by cutting away with an ax or an adze. An adze had a longer handle than an ax, and its blade formed a right angle with the handle. Adzes could make more precise cuts than an ax. An eighteenth-century guidebook for carpenters explained that the tool was used "to take thin chips off timber or boards, and to take off those **irregularities** that the ax by reason of its form cannot well come at. . . ."

To cut lumber to the right length, a carpenter used a variety of saws. The largest saws required two men to work them, one on either side of the log they were cutting. One of these large

A modern carpenter uses a colonial tool to plane wood.

saws was called a pit saw. One man stood above the log while the other stood in a pit dug beneath it. The pull of gravity helped make the sawing easier for the man in the pit, but harder for the one above the log.

Smaller saws required just one hand, and they came in a variety of sizes. A compass saw had a long, thin blade. After the carpenter drilled out a small hole in the wood, he could insert the compass saw and use it to cut out a larger hole. For small, precise cuts, carpenters used back saws, which had a metal strip over the back of the blade to keep it—and the cut—straight.

Preparing to Build

To get a smooth finish on a piece of wood, the carpenter used a plane. It had a small blade set inside a block of wood, which the carpenter held in both hands. Moving the plane back and forth stripped away thin slices of wood. Carpenters used different planes for different tasks. A molding plane helped the carpenter cut shapes in the wood. A joining plane could cut a groove into which another piece of wood was placed.

For making smaller, precise cuts in wood, the carpenter turned to his gouges and chisels. Both had small metal blades set into wooden handles. One kind of chisel was used to carve away wood and form a mortise and

A variety of carpenters' tools hang on a wall, where they can be easily reached.

tenon joint. A carpenter was more likely to use these tools when making furniture, to create rounded edges or hollow surfaces.

How a piece of wood was used sometimes shaped its final appearance. If a piece of timber would not be seen by anyone, the carpenter did not have to plane it. For a floorboard, for example, the carpenter wanted the visible side smooth, but the underside could be rough. Leaving the two sides in different states was sometimes called putting the "best face to London." This meant impressing visitors with the visible wood while not wasting time on something no one would ever see.

Putting It Together

Once the timbers were cut to the right size and shape, the carpenter had to assemble the pieces. When using mortise and tenon construction, the carpenter used a type of drill called an auger to make a hole through the pieces of wood. Augers came in different sizes for different uses. Basically, an auger was a long metal rod with a pointed end. The rod was attached to a wooden handle. For making a hole in thick wood, the carpenter used a cross-handed auger. Its handle sat across the rod, so the carpenter could use two hands to turn it. The end of the rod was sometimes spiral-shaped, like a screw. Other cross-handed augers had

Tricks of the Trade

Using certain materials in certain ways was not just about saving time. In New England, some barn carpenters put cedar shingles on the rear and clapboard on the front. The rear side also usually faced the north, which often endured the worst weather, such as cold winds and rain. The cedar shingles served a special purpose. The carpenters knew that cedar resists water and other natural elements that cause other woods to rot. The cedar shingles helped keep the barns strong over many years.

straight rods. A carpenter needed great strength to cut a wide or deep hole in thick wood.

For smaller holes, carpenters used tools called gimlets. The gimlet had a wooden handle and rod, like an auger, but it was much smaller. Carpenters sometimes used gimlets to begin a hole where a nail or screw would go. Without this "pilot" hole, the metal nail could split the wood. Carpenters also used two tools together to make certain holes: the brace and bit. The first colonial braces were made of wood, but later ones were made of metal. The brace held the bits, which were sharp metal pieces of different shapes and sizes. The brace was designed to be turned by hand. The carpenter pressed down on the top handle and turned a U-shaped crank in the middle. The turning motion drove the bit into the wood, similar to a modern drill. Today's drills still use different-sized metal bits to do their work.

When attaching pieces of wood to each other, colonial carpenters had several choices. Wooden pegs were common in the early days. Iron nails appeared during the eighteenth century. The nails were cut from a single iron rod and then hammered at one end to form a point. Unlike the nails, the screws used in colonial days did not have pointed ends; these did not appear until the mid-nineteenth century, when machines could easily create both a spiral and a pointed end.

To drive a nail or peg into wood, carpenters swung hammers similar to the ones still used today. They also had special hammers for specific jobs. Wooden hammers, called mallets, clubs, and mauls, were sometimes used to hammer large wooden pieces together. They were also used if a metal hammer might damage a chisel or other tool that the carpenter wanted to strike. A lathing hammer had two distinct ends. One had a blade used to cut small pieces of wood called laths. The laths were used to build walls. The other end of the lathing hammer was used to nail the laths in place.

Hammer heads came in different sizes to match the carpenter's different needs.

A Man of Many Trades

Joshua Hempstead was both a shipwright and a house carpenter, so he would have had a variety of tools. Actually, he was what is sometimes called a "jack-of-all-trades." He performed many jobs for his neighbors and on his own farm, as his diary shows:

September 8, 1711: "I worked at the ship about the stern. . . ."

September 10, 1711: "I went to work . . . for Joseph Truman at his house for him to make a pair of shoes. . . ."

September 20, 1711: "I mowed and put in Joseph Truman's windows in the forenoon and in the afternoon I went to get timber for the belfry. . . ."

July 31, 1718: "I was in town and bought 516 foot white pine boards . . . I fetched home the boards in the whale boat."

October 9, 1721: "I was home all day stacking hay. I finished [making] the ferryman's oars."

October 12, 1721: "I mended Mr. Winthrop's wheel that Stephen broke the day before yesterday carting a load [of] wood."

Other Tools of the Trade

Devices for sawing, shaping, drilling, and hammering formed the largest part of the carpenter's toolbox. But he also relied on other tools to do his job as well as possible. Measuring and leveling wood required several tools. A measuring stick, or ruler, made out of wood was marked off in inches. A tool called a square formed a 90-degree angle. Carpenters used it to mark lumber to make square cuts and to make sure two walls met accurately in a corner. An iron square was sometimes marked off in inches, giving the carpenter another ruler for measuring. Carpenters also used the tools of mathematicians, such as protractors to measure angles and compasses to plot curves.

A man dressed as a colonial carpenter makes a window sash, which was used to hold glass in place.

Another measuring device was a caliper. A carpenter measured the width of a piece of wood with its thin "arms." He could then lock the arms in place and move the caliper to duplicate the same width on another piece of wood.

A level, like a square, helped a carpenter tell if the wood was aligned just right. The earliest levels had a piece of metal tied

Colonial carpenters used mallets like these when working with certain pieces of wood.

to string. This was called a plumb bob. It was attached to a piece of curved wood nailed to a flat piece of wood. The level was placed on a board. If the plumb bob did not line up with the middle of the flat, bottom piece of wood, then the board it sat on was not level.

To put a large house together, a carpenter needed a pike. This long pole with a metal hook on it helped raise up the frame. For even bigger jobs, he would turn to a gin pole, which has been called an eighteenth-century crane. The single pole was held in place by ropes and had pulleys on it that could lift up taller, heavier frames.

Acquiring Tools

For most of the colonial era, a carpenter could make his own tools, or at least parts of them. Many of the tools were made from wood. A carpenter who knew something about metal work could make the parts that needed to be iron. But most carpenters turned to another skilled craftsman, the blacksmith, for their metal tools and nails. If no blacksmith was nearby, carpenters had to rely on getting metal tools from merchants or neighbors who traveled to towns large enough to have a blacksmith. Some craftsmen preferred to get tools that were made in England. The English smiths were usually more skilled and had cheaper prices. Their tools lasted longer than many that were made in America.

Some carpenters also received tools as payment from their customers. Paper money was not used, and even coins were scarce in some parts of the colonies. At different times and in different places, Americans used tobacco or corn as forms of money. Many farmers and artisans traded goods or services with each other to pay what they owed. The records of the Dominy family of Long Island show that Isaac Barns paid his bill with gimlets, while another customer paid with a plane. Over time, a carpenter's tools wore out or broke, so fixing or replacing them was always a concern. But a good carpenter, with plenty of work, could afford that expense. And having the best tools possible made his job easier.

Blacksmiths used metal hammers and a special platform called an anvil to make carpenters' tools and other metal items.

FOUR

Carpenters and Their Communities

Carpenters relied on the help of many people to complete their jobs. They had the apprentices and journeymen who worked underneath them. They hired laborers, sometimes slaves, to do the heaviest lifting. On large jobs, they arranged for other skilled craftsmen to do brickwork or complete the inside of a building. For a house in Williamsburg, Virginia, a carpenter and the men he worked with might spend a year together to complete the job.

But a carpenter did not spend all his time at a work site. Some carpenters also spent time with other carpenters in social gatherings. Together, the carpenters talked about their craft and how to get the best rates for their work. They also took part in the larger community, sometimes playing an important role in local politics.

A team of carpenters works together to put up the frame of a house.

The Carpenters' Company

Today, workers in the same profession sometimes join a union. The union works to help them get the best pay and working conditions. The guilds of England were an early form of a union. Working together, artisans with similar skills could best protect their interests. Although colonial artisans did not bring the guild system to America, they sometimes formed groups that looked out for the interests of everyone who shared a skill.

For most of the eighteenth century, Philadelphia was the grandest city in the colonies. Wealthy merchants built impressive homes and helped pay for public buildings. All that construction meant plenty of work for carpenters. They flocked to the city from Boston, New York, and overseas. The carpenters already in Philadelphia wanted some control over their trade, to make sure they had enough work and were paid fairly. To address their concerns, they formed the Company of Carpenters of Philadelphia. Begun during the 1720s, the group was also called the Carpenters' Company.

The Philadelphia Carpenters' Company was similar to one in London that was several hundred years old. The London company was designed to protect the "mystery and brotherhood" of carpentry. It required anyone who wanted to practice carpentry in London to have served as an apprentice for seven years. Then the carpenter had to win the approval of the company's leaders to practice his craft. Philadelphia's Carpenters' Company was not so strict. A person could be a carpenter in the city without joining the company. But the best Philadelphia carpenters did belong, and they did most of the major building jobs in the city.

The Carpenters' Company said it was formed "for the purpose of obtaining instruction in the science of architecture." Another goal was to help members who needed medical care if they were hurt on the job. Any work that required handling sharp tools

A Member of the Company

Benjamin Loxley belonged to the Carpenters' Company. He wrote a short autobiography that described some of his life as a carpenter: "He [Loxley's uncle] bound [indentured] me for five years to W. Joseph Watkins, where I learned the carpenter's, joiner's and plain cabinet making trades. They used me exceeding kind. I was free May 7, 1742. I worked journey work for my master about two months, then joined partnership with William Henderson. . . . I had a choice chest of tools . . . the tools were saws, augers, bits, axes, adzes, etc. . . . I went on quite well and got plenty of work and good pay. . . ."

Loxley's notes also seem to reveal when the Carpenters' Company was founded. Some sources say it was in 1724, but he recorded that the company began in February 1727.

Joiners, such as Loxley and this modern-day carpenter, assembled many different items out of wood.

or lifting heavy weights, as a carpenter's job did, could lead to serious accidents. Carpenters also had to work on ladders, which could be dangerous. In his diary, Joshua Hempstead described how one worker "fell down of from [*sic*] a ladder . . . and like[ly] to have broke his leg." But the Carpenters' Company was mainly concerned with getting its members the best work at the best pay.

A Historic Time

Over the decades, members of the Carpenters' Company became close to some of Philadelphia's wealthy merchants. The best carpenters became rich themselves, and some served in the city government. Most of the company's members were master builders, not journeymen or carpenters with a small shop. Yet, because they hired so many artisans and laborers, the company carpenters also kept in touch with the "common man." They knew the interests and concerns of most Philadelphians.

In 1770, the Carpenters' Company began building a hall. The members wanted to show off their building skills and provide a space Philadelphians could rent for special events. The two-story brick hall was completed in 1774, and soon became the site of important political activity.

Building the Hall

The Carpenters' Hall is considered a great example of 1770s colonial architecture. The basement was dug out by hand, with workers using picks and shovels. The foundation was made of stone, and the first floor rested on two massive wooden beams, each 45 feet long. Mortise and tenon joints were used to lock together timbers. To help fireproof the building, the carpenters borrowed an idea from Philadelphia's most famous citizen, Ben Franklin. The inventor and statesman suggested covering wooden laths with plaster and putting them under the floor. The plaster resisted fire, and it also helped keep sound from traveling between the floors. Carpenters' Hall still stands today, and it receives about 150,000 visitors each year.

Parts of Carpenters' Hall were later used as a bank and classrooms.

In December 1773, men in Boston—including several carpenters—had thrown hundreds of crates of tea into the harbor. They were protesting a British tax on tea, after years of arguing with the British over other taxes. Great Britain responded to this "Boston Tea Party" by shutting down the harbor and ending local political control in Massachusetts. In Philadelphia and other cities, **patriots** met to debate how to respond to the British actions. They wanted to show support for Boston and challenge British policies they disliked.

Robert Smith was one of several members of the Carpenters' Company who took an interest in these political events. Smith served on the committee that kept in touch with Boston patriots. Through the summer of 1774, he and other Philadelphia patriots met at Carpenters' Hall to discuss what to do next. Another group met at the nearby State House. The group at Carpenters' Hall tended to be more vocal in supporting the patriots who were attacking British policies.

On September 5, Carpenters' Hall was chosen as the site for a historic political event. **Delegates** from twelve colonies met there to discuss united action against the British. This came to be called the First Continental Congress, and it marked a major step on the road to American independence from Great Britain.

Carpenters and the War

Robert Smith was not the only colonial carpenter to side with the patriots in the battle for independence. In Virginia, master builder Benjamin Powell had become one of Williamsburg's leading citizens. In 1774, he served on a committee that enforced a local law calling on Virginians not to buy British goods. Once the American Revolution started, Virginia hired Powell to build **barracks** for local troops.

Not every carpenter who helped with the war effort was as successful as Powell. Alexander Hoy also lived in Williamsburg, but he struggled to support his family. By the 1760s, he owed money that he could not pay. In 1776, he joined the military, perhaps as much for the money as for his belief in the cause. Hoy served for several years, part of the time under General George Washington.

Boston patriots come out to hear a public reading of the Declaration of Independence in 1776.

Like other Americans, not all carpenters united behind the patriots. Some thought it was their duty to remain loyal to Great Britain and its king. John Nutting, a carpenter from Massachusetts, was one of these loyalists. In 1774 or 1775, Nutting hired men to help him build barracks for the British troops stationed in Boston. As a British report later noted, "this conduct made him very obnoxious to his countrymen . . . at one time he was seized on his way to his own house and ill used [mistreated] by the Rebels. . . . his conduct in **procuring** workmen and carrying out the public works made him so disagreeable to the people of Boston, that he could not stir without a guard."

Carpenters, like other colonial Americans, had a wide range of backgrounds and views. But whether they were patriots or loyalists, from the North or from the South, they had something in common. Carpenters had the skills and the tools to help build a growing nation.

Glossary

apprentice   young person who lives and works with someone who is expert in a particular craft

artisans   people with great skill in a particular craft done by hand

barracks   buildings where soldiers live

belfry   a tower in a building, often a bell tower

clapboard   long piece of wood used to cover the outside of a building

colonies   lands not connected to a nation, yet owned and controlled by it

delegates   people chosen to represent a larger group's views at a meeting

geometry   branch of math that deals with points, lines, shapes, and angles

indentures   special contracts that spelled out the duties of masters and their apprentices

irregularities   things that are not normal or desirable

patriots   colonial Americans who opposed some British laws and later supported independence from Great Britain

Pilgrims   English settlers who landed in Plymouth, Massachusetts, in 1620

plantations   large farms where usually one main crop is grown, often by slaves

procuring   hiring or obtaining

rafters   beams used to support a roof

shipwrights   carpenters who specialize in building ships

statesman   a respected government official, often one who represents his country overseas

thatcher   a person who makes roofs out of straw or other plant material

timbers   pieces of wood used in construction

Find Out More

BOOKS

Krebs, Laurie. *A Day in the Life of a Colonial Shipwright.* New York: PowerKids Press, 2004.

Pederson, Charles E. *The Jamestown Colony.* Edina, MN: ABDO, 2009.

Sherman, Patrice. *Colonial America.* Hockessin, DE: Mitchell Lane Publishers, 2010.

WEBSITES

Carpenters' Hall

http://www.ushistory.org/carpentershall/index.htm

Colonial House

http://www.pbs.org/wnet/colonialhouse/

Colonial Williamsburg—Carpenters and Joiners

http://www.history.org/almanack/life/trades/tradecar.cfm

Plimoth Plantation

http://www.plimoth.org/

Index

Page numbers in **boldface** are illustrations.

About the Author

Michael Burgan has written more than 250 books for children and young adults, both fiction and nonfiction. He specializes in American history and has written several books about the colonial and Revolutionary era, including *Voices from Colonial America: New York*; *Colonial and Revolutionary Times*; and biographies of John Winthrop, Samuel Adams, and Thomas Paine. A graduate of the University of Connecticut with a degree in history, Burgan has won several awards for his writing. He currently lives in New Mexico.